There's a Hand in the Sky

There's a Hand in the Sky

OSCAR DE MEJO

PANTHEON BOOKS

ALSO BY OSCAR DE MEJO
The Tiny Visitor

Published in the United States by Pantheon Books, a division of Random House, Inc., New York,
and simultaneously in Canada by Random House of Canada Limited, Toronto.
Designed by Mimi Harrison
Manufactured in the United States of America
1 3 5 7 9 0 8 6 4 2
First Edition

Library of Congress Cataloging in Publication Data
De Mejo, Oscar. There's a hand in the sky.
Summary: The ghost of a Pomona, California, millionaire invites two children
to be his guests at a splendid masked ball, first giving them the secret
of his hidden wealth to pass on to his recently impoverished heirs.
[1. Ghosts—Fiction. 2. California—Fiction. 3. Inheritance and succession—Fiction. 4. Parties—Fiction]
I. Title. PZ7.D3396Th 1983 [E] 83-2320
ISBN 0-394-85667-8 ISBN 0-394-95667-2 (lib. bdg.)

To my two sons, Carlo and Larry

LONG, LONG AGO, Lady Luck was a frequent visitor to Pomona, California.

Gwyneth and Elizabeth, two sisters, were among the luckiest people in Pomona. They and their husbands, Theophilus and Robert, had inherited the vast fortune of Captain Homer McMillan Solo.

The two couples made their home in the McMillan mansion, where they enjoyed a happy and carefree life

until, suddenly and unexpectedly, Lady Luck turned her back on them and went away.

The bank where Gwyneth and Elizabeth kept all their money burned down to the ground

and the bank where Theophilus and Robert kept their own fortunes was robbed by some very determined bandits.

Gwyneth and Theophilus, Elizabeth and Robert had lost everything.

"We'll have to sell the mansion," said Theophilus.
"What else can we do?" said Robert.

Gwyneth and Elizabeth, heartbroken, were forced to agree. To cheer them up, their husbands proposed that they give one last party—a spectacular masked ball— before selling the mansion.

As they went to make the arrangements, they didn't notice that a hand in the sky was trying to give them a letter.

Not far from the McMillan mansion lived two children, Mic and Beshamel.

Their mother, Lucinda, loved them dearly and spanked them often. She had a particular talent, washing clothes. People came from afar to see her hang the laundry—it was so incredibly clean.

Their father, Fabritius, worked in his shop on Solo Street, making beautiful furniture. He was known throughout Pomona for his elegance, and people called him "the gentleman carpenter."

On the way to school every morning, Mic and Beshamel passed the McMillan mansion, and told each other stories about the famous sisters and their legendary wealth.

The day before the masked ball, they imagined the splendid costumes and lavish entertainment that would be seen in the mansion the following night.

At school, the children talked of nothing else. Of course no children were going to the party, since it would not begin until ten o'clock in the evening.

As Mic lay in bed that night,

the door of his room opened and a ghostly figure came in.

"I am Captain Homer McMillan Solo," the figure said gravely, "and I came to tell you that you must go to the ball my daughters are giving tomorrow—" he winked, and added—"whether you are invited or not." And he disappeared.

On the way to school the next morning, Mic was telling Beshamel about his strange dream when she interrupted him. "There's a hand in the sky," she said. At first, deep in thought, Mic didn't pay attention.

But then the hand came down from the sky and offered them an envelope. Beshamel took it, and the hand disappeared.

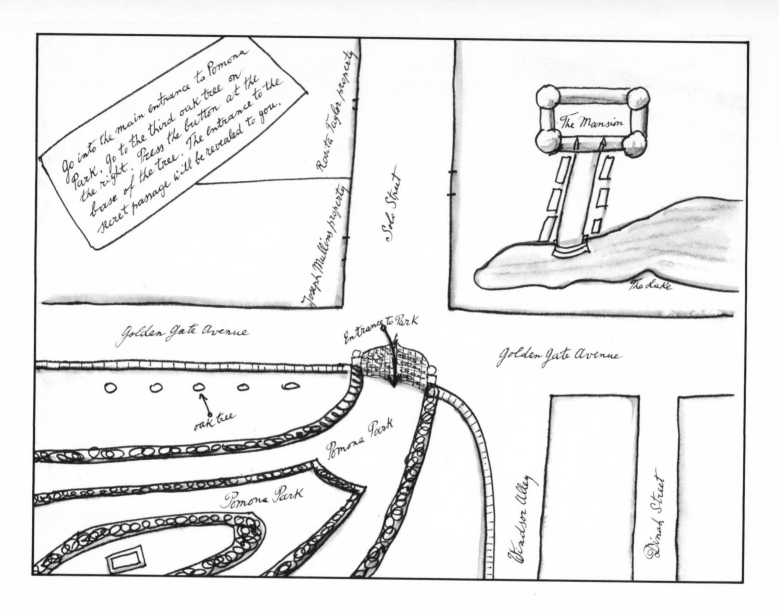

The envelope contained a map and a brief message. It said: "Go into the main entrance to Pomona Park. Go to the third oak tree on the right. Press the button at the base of the tree. The entrance to the secret passage will be revealed to you."

They studied the map. "The secret passage must lead to the mansion," said Mic. "So we *can* go to the ball," said Beshamel. "But we need disguises."

"If I wear a false moustache, people will think I am a middle-aged gentleman dressed as a child," said Mic. "And if you wear a mask, people will think you are a very short lady dressed as a little girl."

That night, Mic and Beshamel were unusually quiet at dinner. When Mic said he wanted to go to bed early, their mother was pleased.

At 10:30, Mic and Beshamel crept quietly from their rooms.

The night was silent and mysterious.

They had to pass the ancient cemetery…

and finally they reached the entrance to Pomona Park.

They turned right and counted three big oak trees. "Here is the button," said Mic.

He pressed it and a door opened in the trunk of the tree.

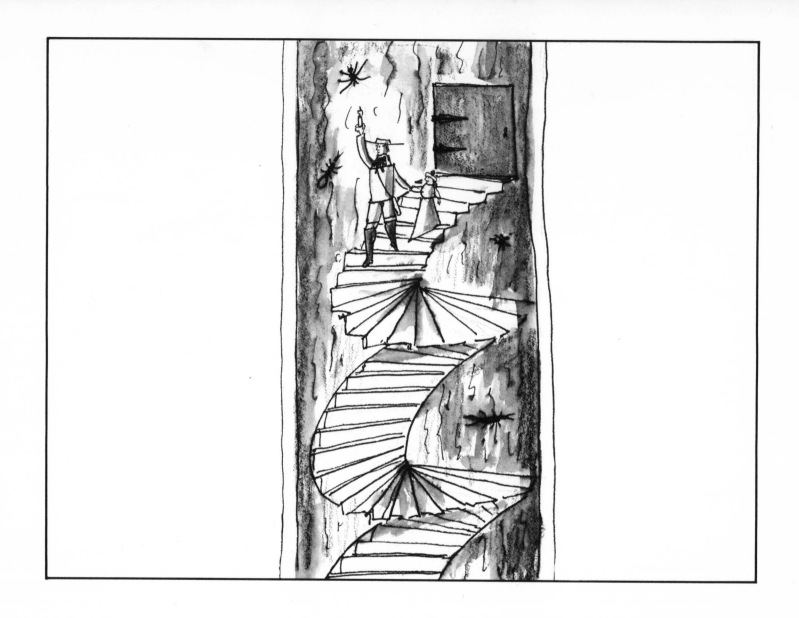

Inside was a spiral staircase. As they started to descend, the door closed behind them with a clang.

At the bottom of the staircase they entered a long tunnel.

It led into another tunnel, and another,

which opened into a large room. There was a lot of gold lined up against the wall. "This must be where they keep their treasure," said Beshamel.

Mic opened a door that led to a flight of stairs. From above came a faint sound of music.

At the top of the stairs, they went through a little door and were faced with a marvelous spectacle. The masquerade was in full swing.

They saw Mr. and Mrs. Carpenter, who had come dressed as an armchair; Mr. Howard Baltic, who impersonated Mount Vesuvius; and Miss Millicent Clark, who was dressed as an umbrella.

Mrs. Mary Lou Bartlett was a pencil, the three brothers Amoroso were an ocean clipper, and Miss Barbara Otis, the schoolteacher, was disguised as a bunch of grapes.

Miss Priscilla Longfellow was a huge ladybug, young Mr. Peter Potter was a moon-lit landscape with clouds, and rotund Dr. Sam Bobicek was an oversized pocket watch.

Bizarre Mr. Marvin McAdam came disguised as a big head on wheels; Miss Anita Furlough, the dancer, was made up as a luscious chocolate mousse; and Sir Rebozo Avis wore a bird costume.

Mic and Beshamel went into the library to discuss their plans. Tired from their journey and the late hour, they fell asleep. They slept until the party was over and all the guests had gone…

and awoke to find four masked figures standing before them. "I am Robert," said one, "and these are Gwyneth and Theophilus and Elizabeth. Who are you?"

Mic and Beshamel bowed respectfully, and Mic's moustache fell off. "We are Mic and Beshamel," he said.

They all sat down in the drawing room. "How did you get here?" asked Gwyneth.

"Through the secret passage," said Mic.

"And the treasure room," said Beshamel.

Their hosts and hostesses were astonished. When Mic and Beshamel described the gold, there was general rejoicing.

They all rushed into the ballroom to look for the door to the secret passage, but the elusive door was nowhere to be found.

So they all went out into Pomona Park

and through the little door in the oak tree.

Mic and Beshamel easily led the sisters and their husbands to the treasure room.

Gwyneth, Elizabeth, Theophilus, and Robert were overjoyed. They gave Mic and Beshamel a large reward for finding the gold, and the coachman drove them home.

Their parents were delighted. Their father opened a precious fifty-year-old bottle of French champagne to celebrate. "Where is Beshamel?" he asked.

At that moment the door opened and Beshamel rushed in. "There's a hand in the sky," she said.

This time, the hand was formed by little birds

who rearranged themselves

to form a message: THANKS.

"You're welcome," said Mic and Beshamel.

OSCAR DE MEJO

was born in Trieste, Italy, into a family of music enthusiasts. After obtaining doctoral degrees in both law and social science he came to Hollywood, where his first job was as a composer. Following a brief but successful career in music he turned to painting, and in 1950 had a one-man show at the Carlebach Gallery in New York City. Since that time, Mr. de Mejo's work has been shown throughout the U.S. and Europe, and has been commissioned by many private collectors, organizations, and magazines. He is the artist/author of *My America* (Abrams, 1983) and of *The Tiny Visitor,* judged one of the ten best illustrated children's books of 1982 by *The New York Times,* in which the two rich sisters from Pomona made their debut.